MW00987942

Welcome to "ASL Fingerspelling Practice," a captivating journey into the world of American Sign Language (ASL) through the art of word search puzzles!

———————

This unique and engaging book is crafted to provide a fun and educational way to practice identifying ASL alphabet letters and finger-spelled words.

———————

Whether you're a beginner eager to learn the basics or an experienced signer looking to enjoy some word search fun our puzzles offers a diverse range of words to challenge and expand your skill in identifying ASL alphabet letters.

———————

From everyday expressions to unique and thematic terms, each puzzle has been simply designed to incorporate a variety of words, providing an immersive and enjoyable learning experience.

Themed puzzles

These puzzles not only enhance your ASL alphabet recognition but also introduce you to the visual language associated with

everyday themes. Immerse yourself in the joy of spotting ASL letters within words that resonate with familiar and captivating topics.

Positive Affirmation Word Searches

Embrace the power of positivity as you navigate through grids filled with encouraging statements, making your ASL journey not just educational but also empowering.

These 11x11 Affirmation puzzles are designed to boost your confidence and inspire a positive mindset while honing your efforts to quickly identify the affirmation statement within the puzzle.

BASEBALL

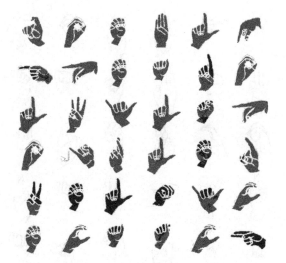

BALL

GLOVE   CATCH

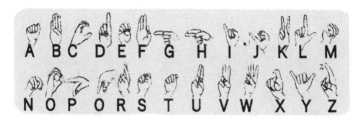

CARS

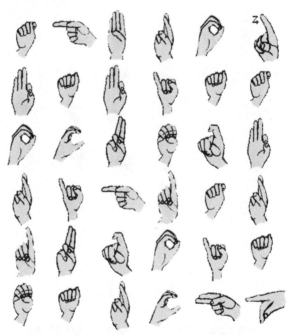

AUDI   FIAT   FORD

CATS

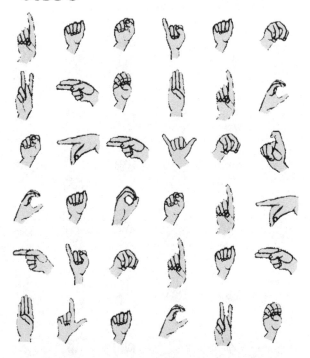

ASIAN BLACK SPHYNX

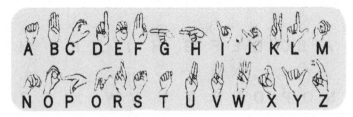

FURNITURE

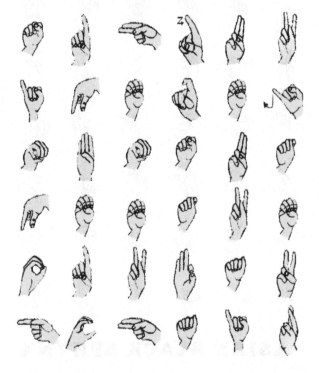

BED   DESK   CHAIR

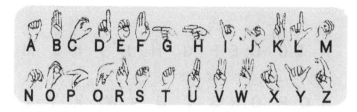

SCHOOL SUBJECTS

ART

MUSIC   **MATH**

COLORS

BEIGE   OLIVE   NAVY

TREES

BIRCH CEDAR SPRUCE

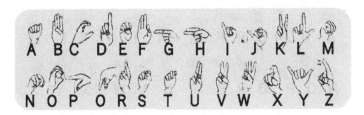

FOOTWARE

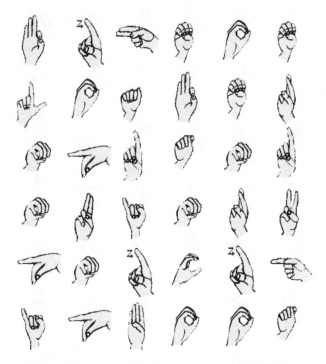

BOOT   PUMP   LOAFER

CITIES

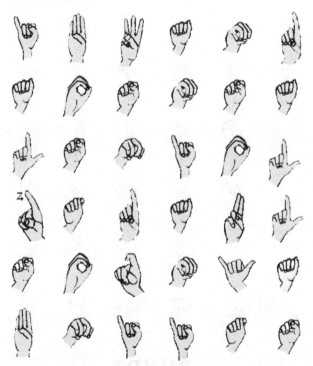

BOSTON   MIAMI   DALLAS

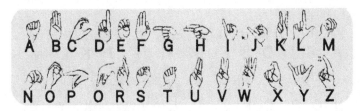

CAKES

BUNDT

POUND   LAYER

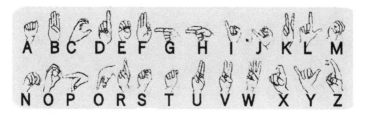

DESSERTS

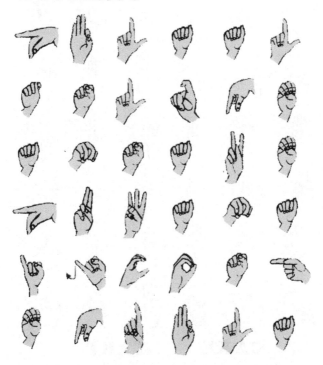

CAKE PIE FLAN

DESSERTS

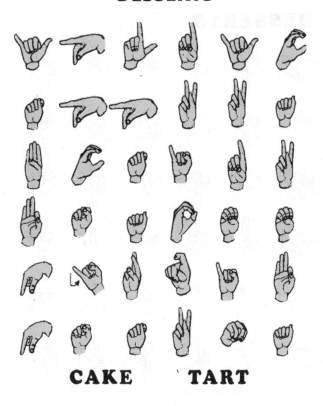

CAKE   **TART**

PIE

INSTRUMENTS

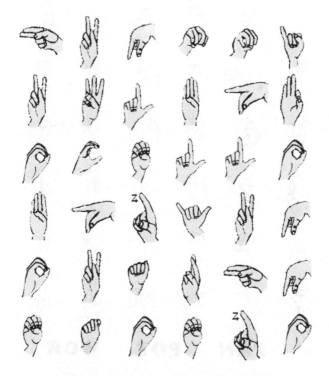

CELLO OBOE LYRE

COOKWARE

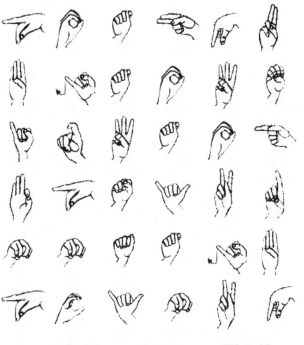

PAN   POT   WOK

APPLIANCES

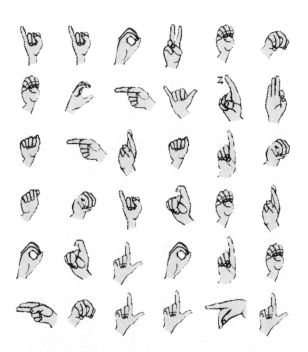

OVEN GRILL MIXER

COUNTRIES

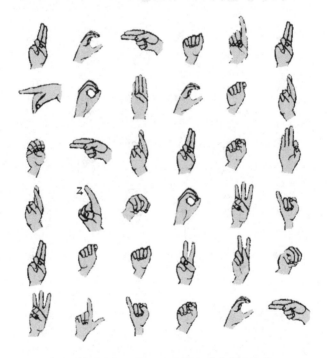

PERU CHAD LAOS

WRITING TOOLS

PEN QUILL CHALK

TREES

WILLOW

PINE **OAK**

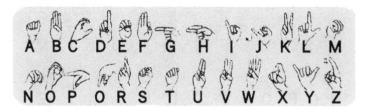

DANCES

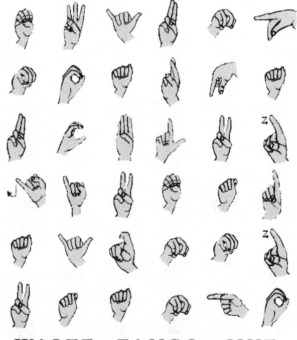

WALTZ TANGO JIVE

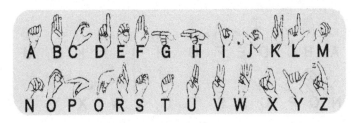

A B C D E F G H I J K L M
N O P Q R S T U V W X Y Z

FLOWERS

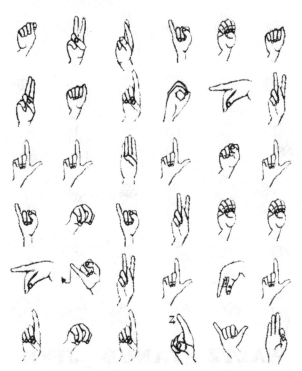

TULIP LILY ROSE

DRINKS

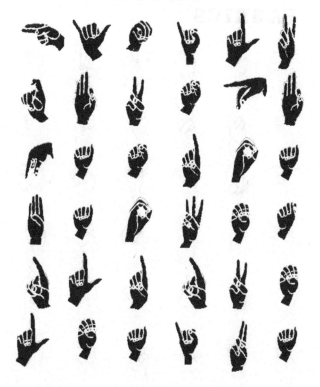

TEA SODA MILK

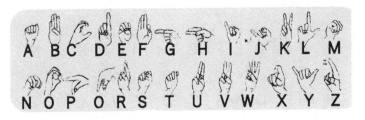

FABRICS

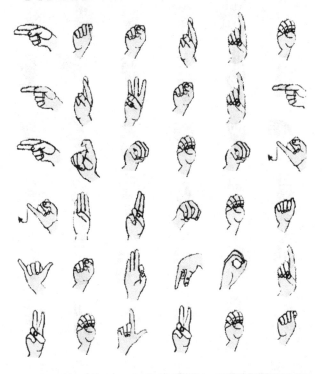

SUEDE TWEED VELVET

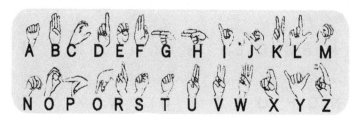

A B C D E F G H I J K L M
N O P Q R S T U V W X Y Z

SPACE

STAR COMET ORION

FABRICS

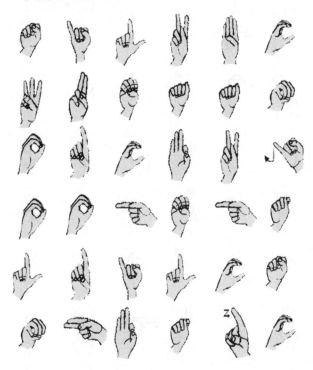

SILK WOOL FELT

A B C D E F G H I J K L M

N O P Q R S T U V W X Y Z

TREES

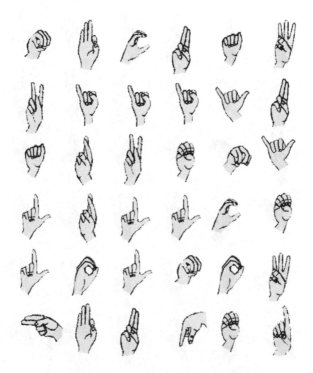

FIR   ELM   YEW

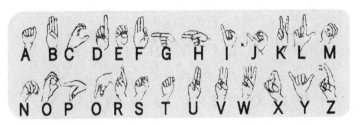

BIRDS

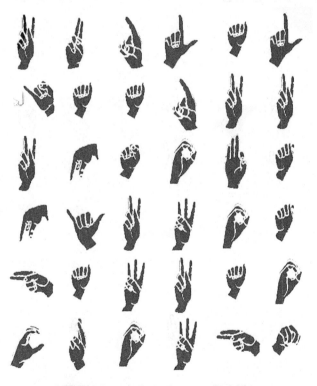

CROW HAWK SWAN

SHAPES

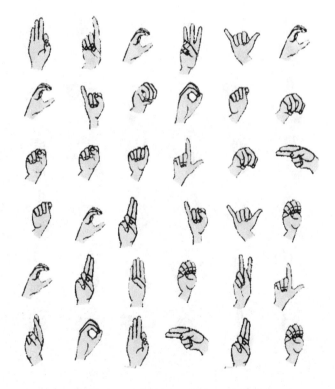

CUBE CONE DISC

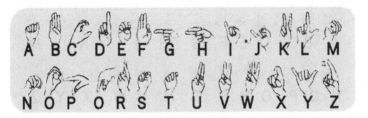

CEREALS

CORN RICE OATS

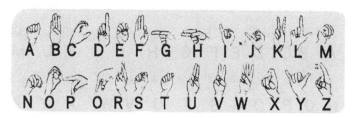

FISH

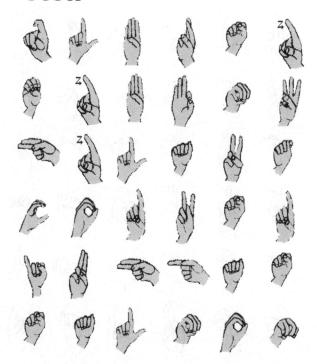

COD SALMON BASS

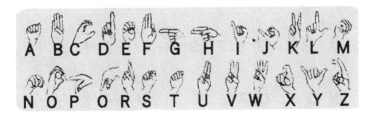

CHEESE

CREAM BLUE GOUDA

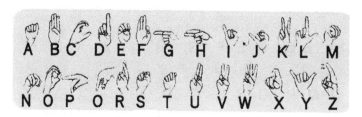

DRINKS

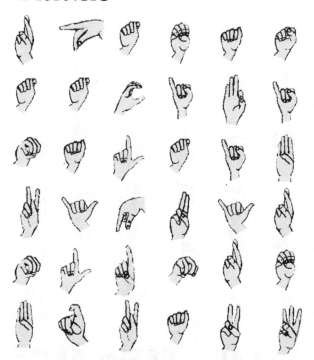

MALT TEA BREW

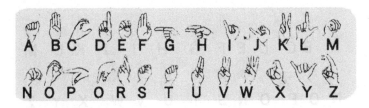

FABRICS

LACE   DENIM   SATIN

COSMETICS

MASK TINT BALM

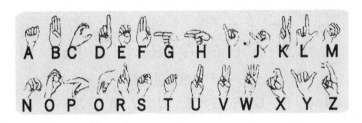

CARS

MINI SEDAN CHEVY

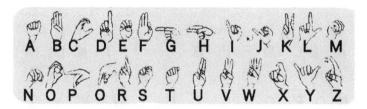

HERBS

MINT BASIL THYME

WEATHER

MIST SLEET FROST

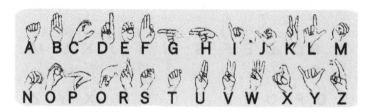

FRUIT

KIWI DATE PLUM

VEETABLES

KALE   LEEK   CORN

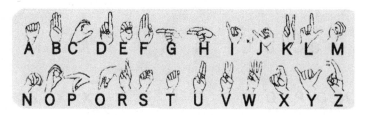

DOGS

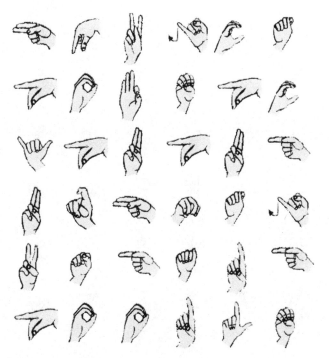

HOUND POODLE PUG

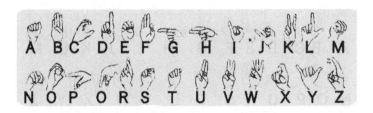

A B C D E F G H I J K L M
N O P Q R S T U V W X Y Z

CURRENCIES

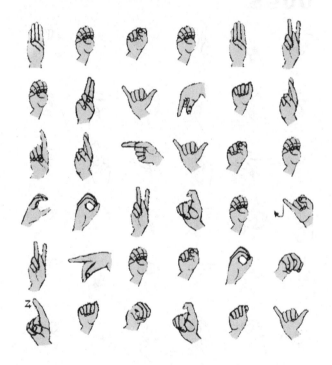

YEN EURO PESO

FABRICS

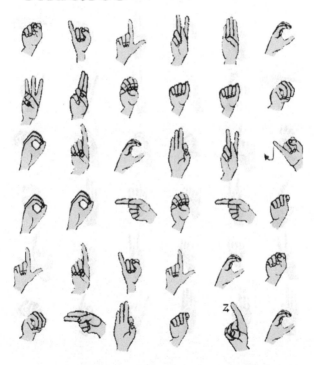

SILK WOOL FELT

TREES

PINE OAK ELM

TEAS

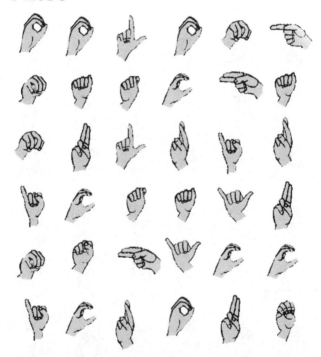

CHAI OOLONG MATCHA

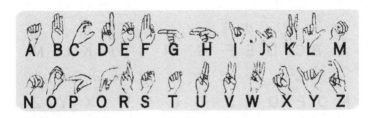

SPICES

CUMIN SALT CLOVE

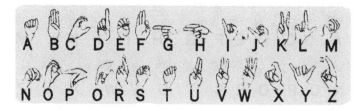

GAMES

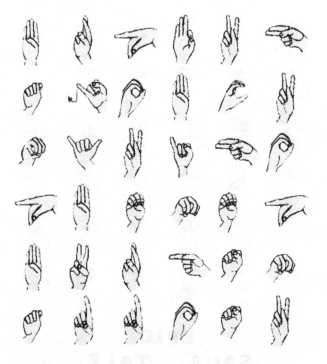

CHESS POKER BINGO

BOOKS

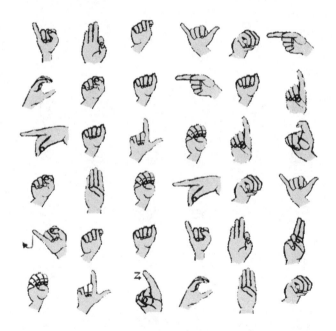

EPIC
SAGA   TALE

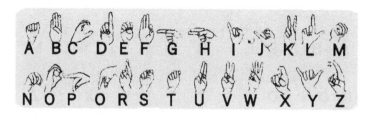

COMPUTER PARTS

CHIP   PORT   FAN

TEMPERATURES

HOT   COLD   WARM

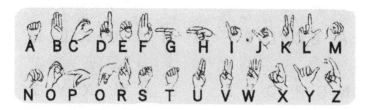

TREES

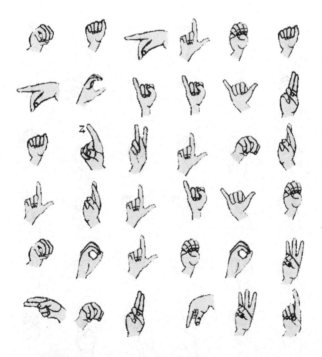

HOLLY MAPLE PALM

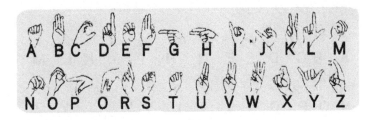

SPICES

SALT   DILL   SAGE

TOOLS

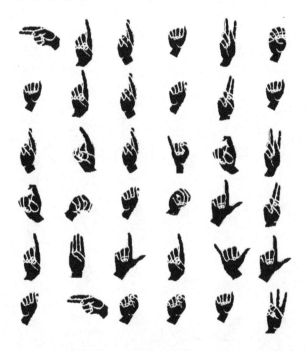

SAW   DRILL   RAKE

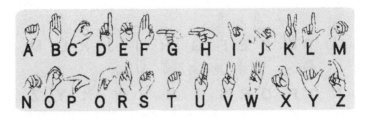

BODIES OF WATER

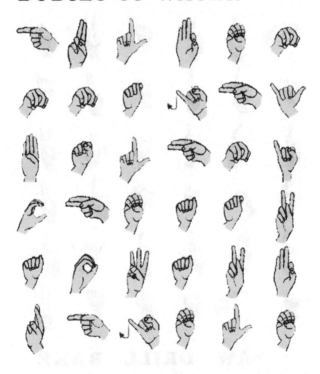

SEA LAKE GULF

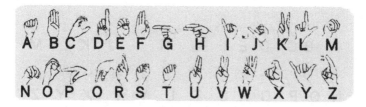

MUSIC

POP **JAZZ** **SOUL**

JEWELRY

RING   CHAIN   BROOCH

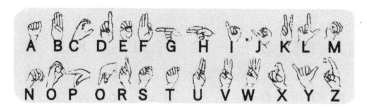

BREADS

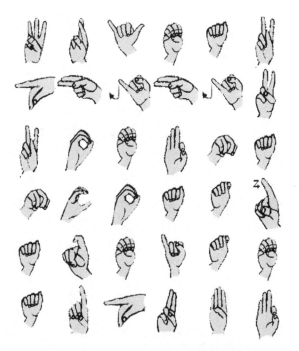

WHEAT
PITA   RYE

FRUIT

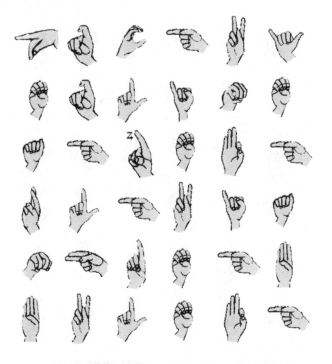

PEAR FIG LIME

BIRDS

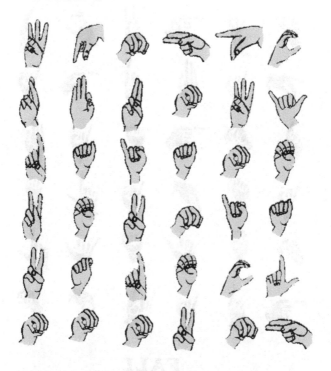

RAVEN FINCH QUAIL

A B C D E F G H I J K L M
N O P R S T U V W X Y Z

SEASONS

FALL
SPRING   WINTER

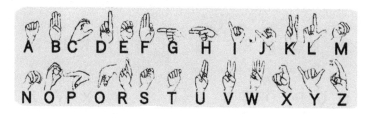

GEMS

OPAL JADE TOPAZ

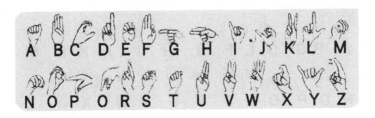

FAMILY

MOM DAD SON

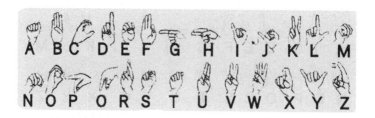

SPORTS

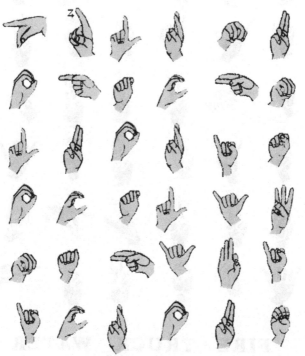

GOLF POLO SWIM

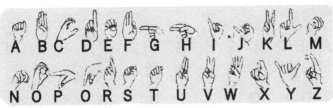

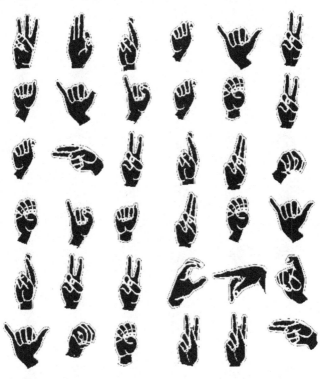

FIRE TRUCK WATER

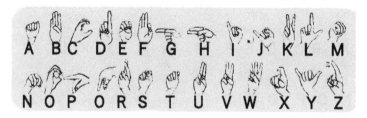

WEATHER

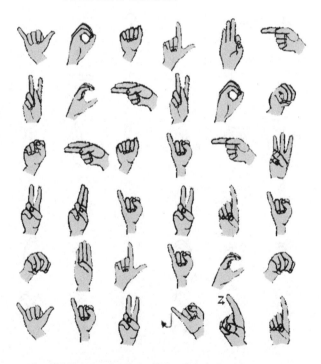

FOG HAIL WIND

COLOES

GOLD   RED   BLUE

Cultivate
inner peace

1:11 Affirmation Puzzle

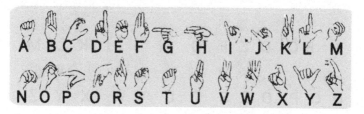

A B C D E F G H I J K L M

N O P Q R S T U V W X Y Z

Celebrate
your uniqueness

11:11 Affirmation Puzzle

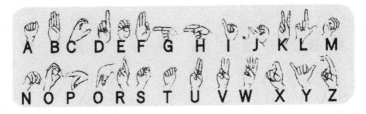

A B C D E F G H I J K L M
N O P Q R S T U V W X Y Z

Positive
mental focus

11:11 Affirmation Puzzle

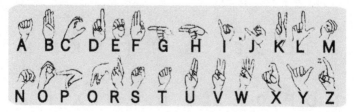

MY THOUGHTS
CREATE VICTORIES

11:11 Affirmation Puzzle

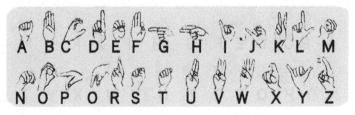

Nurture
your dreams

11:11 Affirmation Puzzle

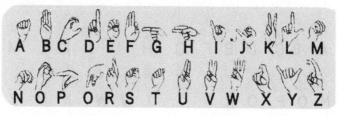

POSITIVITY
IS MY MINDSET

11:11 Affirmation Puzzle

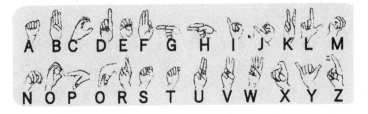

Abundance
flows to me

11:11 Affirmation Puzzle

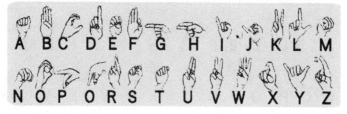

A B C D E F G H I J K L M
N O P Q R S T U V W X Y Z

Celebrate
small victories

11:11 Affirmation Puzzle

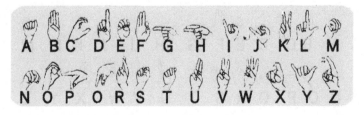

Contribute
Uplift Inspire

11:11 Affirmation Puzzle

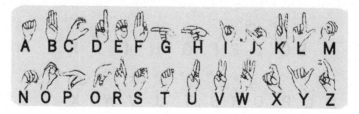

Creativity
flows from within

11:11 Affirmation Puzzle

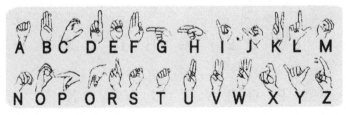

Dream
Believe Achieve

11:11 Affirmation Puzzle

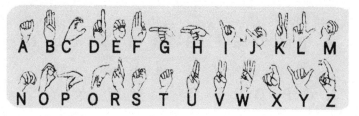

Embrace
Positive Change

11:11 Affirmation Puzzle

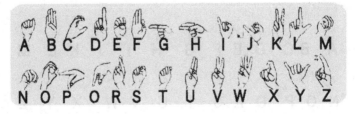

I AM A
SOURCE OF STRENGTH

11:11 Affirmation Puzzle

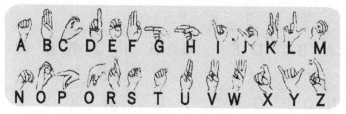

My ideas
are endless

11:11 Affirmation Puzzle

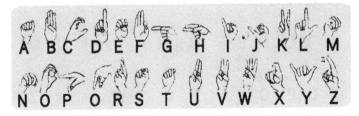

Explore
endless possibility

11:11 Affirmation Puzzle

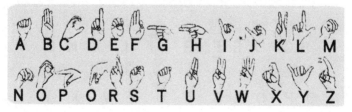

I ATTRACT
GOOD THINGS

11:11 Affirmation Puzzle

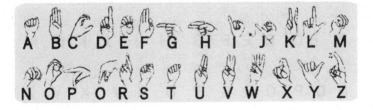

Embrace
Your Power

11:11 Affirmation Puzzle

Overcome obstacles with persistence

11:11 Affirmation Puzzle

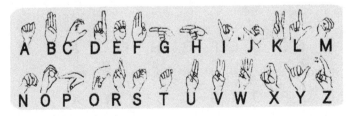

RADIATE
GOOD VIBRATIONS

11:11 Affirmation Puzzle

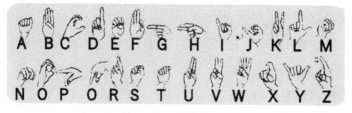

Savor
each triumph

11:11 Affirmation Puzzle

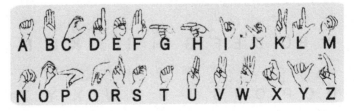

A B C D E F G H I J K L M
N O P Q R S T U V W X Y Z

Soar
with purpose

11:11 Affirmation Puzzle

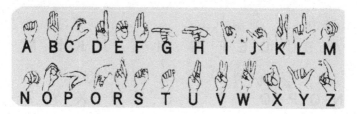

Strength
comes from within

11:11 Affirmation Puzzle

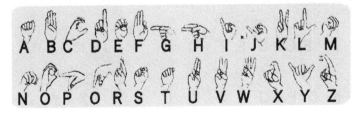

A B C D E F G H I J K L M
N O P Q R S T U V W X Y Z

SUCCESS
IS MY JOURNEY

11:11 Affirmation Puzzle

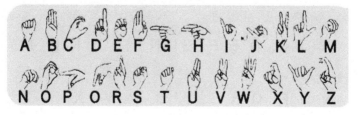

Trust
your instinct

11:11 Affirmation Puzzle

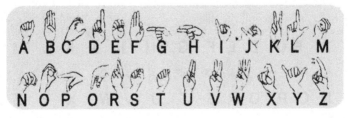

Wisdom
guides my choices

11:11 Affirmation Puzzle

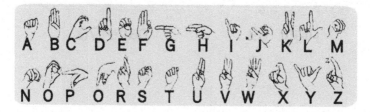

Cultivate
inner peace

page 67

Celebrate
your uniqueness

page 68

Positive
mental focus

page 69

MY THOUGHTS
CREATE VICTORIES

page 70

Nurture
your dreams

page 71

POSITIVITY
IS MY MINDSET

page 72

Abundance
flows to me

page 73

Celebrate
small victories

page 74

**Contribute
Uplift Inspire**

page 75

**Creativity
flows from within**

page 76

**Dream
Believe Achieve**

page 77

**Embrace
Positive Change**

page 78

**I AM A
SOURCE OF STRENGTH**

page 79

**My ideas
are endless**

page 80

**Explore
endless possibility**

page 81

**I ATTRACT
GOOD THINGS**

page 82

**Embrace
Your Power**

page 83

**Overcome obstacles
with persistence**

page 84

**RADIATE
GOOD VIBRATIONS**

page 85

**Savor
each triumph**

page 86

Soar
with purpose

page 87

Strength
comes from within

page 88

SUCCESS
IS MY JOURNEY

page 89

Trust
your instinct

page 90

Wisdom
guides my choices

page 91

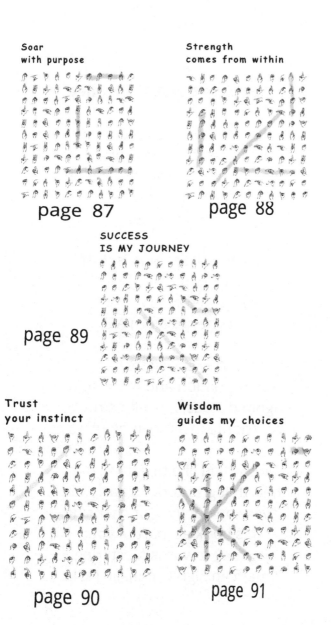

LEARNING ASL With Riley

The decision to create this unique word search practice book was inspired by a deeply personal and meaningful experience.

My grandson, who is deaf, along with my daughter, has embarked on a beautiful journey to learn ASL.

Witnessing their determination and enthusiasm ignited a passion within me to contribute in a meaningful way.

We would like to extend our heartfelt gratitude to each and every one of you for choosing this book as part of your journey towards mastering American Sign Language (ASL).

Made in the USA
Monee, IL
22 November 2024

70955862R00057